Companion Workl

For

Maybe You Should Take to Someone

By

Lori Gottlieb

Book Nerd

Table of Contents

Note to readers:
This is an unofficial companion workbook of Lori Gottlieb's Maybe you should talk to someone. This workbook is designed to enrich your reading experience and help you put the principles into action. Buy the original book here: https://www.amazon.com/Maybe-You-Should-Talk-Someone/dp/1328662055/

Introduction

Use this journal to write down your thoughts and feelings on each chapter as you read the book. Think about how Lori's life relates to your life, and reflect on her clients' experiences. Share your thoughts with other people, and have a great time journaling.

Chapter One of Maybe you should talk to someone

Do you have a hard time getting close to people? Do you know someone who struggles with this?

Do you feel more connected to people you know well?

Have you ever seen a therapist?

Chapter Two of Maybe you should talk to someone

Have you ever faced a presenting problem or know someone who has? This is a problem that reveals a bigger, underlying life problem.

Have you ever gone through an unexpected breakup like Lori did? Or an unexpected life change?

Chapter Three of Maybe you should talk to someone

Have you ever needed someone to just sit with you and listen to you and your feelings?

Have you ever gone to work while feeling unsettled or depressed?

Chapter Four of Maybe you should talk to someone

What was your first job?

Did you enjoy it?

Chapter Five of Maybe you should talk to someone

Has someone requested something of you that you didn't want to give or something that was hard for you to do?

Chapter Six of Maybe you should talk to someone

What is one crises you have been through? How did you manage it and resolve it?

Chapter Seven of Maybe you should talk to someone

How you ever gotten emotional in front of someone even though you had tried to keep your emotions hidden? How did the person respond?

_____
_____
_____
_____
_____
_____
_____

Chapter Eight of Maybe you should talk to someone

Have you ever felt overwhelmed by your emotions? How did you feel?

_____
_____
_____
_____
_____
_____
_____

Chapter Nine of Maybe you should talk to someone

Does it take you a long time to get to know someone?

Chapter Ten of Maybe you should talk to someone

Do you treat yourself with love and respect?

Do you hold people at an arm's distance?

Have you ever faced an issue that was only the tip of the iceberg of a much larger issue?

Chapter Eleven of Maybe you should talk to someone

Notes and Reflections:

Chapter Twelve of Maybe you should talk to someone

Have you ever arrived at the wrong destination in life and decided to make the most of it?

Chapter Thirteen of Maybe you should talk to someone

If you have kids, have you ever had to explain something difficult to them?

Have you ever had a tough conversation or needed to have a talk with someone?

Chapter Fourteen of Maybe you should talk to someone

Have you ever felt divided about your career or wondered which path you should take?

Chapter Fifteen of Maybe you should talk to someone

Do you know someone who has a hard time expressing his or her feelings?

Do you have a hard time expressing how you feel to others?

Chapter Sixteen of Maybe you should talk to someone

Notes and Reflections:

Chapter Seventeen of Maybe you should talk to someone

Notes and Reflections:

Chapter Eighteen of Maybe you should talk to someone

Have you ever had to end a professional relationship?

Chapter Nineteen of Maybe you should talk to someone

Do you have any abandonment issues?

What type of dreams do you get? Do your dreams reflect your fears?

Chapter Twenty of Maybe you should talk to someone

What is one decision you have come to regret? Have you come to accept it? Acceptance is healthy.

| |
| |
| |
| |
| |
| |
| |

Chapter Twenty-One of Maybe you should talk to someone

Do you struggle with any issues?

Is there a relationship you'd like to improve?

Chapter Twenty-Two of Maybe you should talk to someone

Have you ever felt like you were imprisoning yourself and that the exit was just a few feet away?

Are you proactive in making changes in your life?

Chapter Twenty-Three of Maybe you should talk to someone

What is your dream job? Which job would make you feel truly happy and connected?

Have you ever run into someone you didn't want to see?

Chapter Twenty-Four of Maybe you should talk to someone

Have you ever used a dating app or know someone who has? What was your experience like?

What have been some of your best life decisions so far?

Chapter Twenty-Five of Maybe you should talk to someone

What are some accomplishments you're happy with or proud of?

Chapter Twenty-Six of Maybe you should talk to someone

What are you enjoying in your life now?

Chapter Twenty-Seven of Maybe you should talk to someone

Have you ever googled someone or your ex? What did you learn? Were you happy with this action?

| |
| |
| |
| |
| |
| |
| |

Chapter Twenty-Eight of Maybe you should talk to someone

Who are the types of people you attract?

| |
| |
| |
| |
| |
| |
| |

What do you think of Charlotte's situation?

Have you ever come to the realization that you need help with something?

Chapter Twenty-Nine of Maybe you should talk to someone

Have you ever projected your emotions onto someone?

Do you keep any secrets from the people you care about?

Chapter Thirty of Maybe you should talk to someone

What do you think of Lori's first therapy session?

| |
| |
| |
| |
| |
| |
| |

Chapter Thirty-One of Maybe you should talk to someone

Do you believe Lori and her ex are more similar than different? Do we attract people who are similar to us on some level?

Do you believe everything happens for a reason, including challenges?

Chapter Thirty-Two of Maybe you should talk to someone

What do you think of Myron's and Rita's relationship?

What do you think Rita's struggles are really about? The real issue isn't her romantic relationships.

Chapter Thirty-Three of Maybe you should talk to someone

Are most of your decisions based on fear or are they based on love?

Have you ever been emotionally triggered by something that Charlotte had been triggered by?

What do you think of the dude in the waiting room?

What are you attracted to?

Do you think Charlotte will date the dude?

Chapter Thirty-Four of Maybe you should talk to someone

Do you think people should "just be" when they have an issue and go with the flow?

Chapter Thirty-Five of Maybe you should talk to someone

Do you show your emotions publicly?

Do you consider yourself to be an emotional person?

Do you curse often? What makes you curse the most (if you do curse)?

Chapter Thirty-Six of Maybe you should talk to someone

Describe a time when your life felt hectic.

What do you think of the outsourcing of feelings and patient care?

Chapter Thirty-Seven of Maybe you should talk to someone

Do you fear uncertainty? Do you sabotage yourself when you are uncertain about something?

Are you most afraid of isolation, lack of meaning, death, or lack of freedom at this point?

Chapter Thirty-Eight of Maybe you should talk to someone

What do you think of John's story?

Have you ever had a hard time sleeping? What do you think caused the insomnia?

Do you show your full range of feelings to the people in your life?

| |
| |
| |
| |
| |

Chapter Thirty-Nine of Maybe you should talk to someone

Do you think Charlotte is improving and taking action?

Chapter Forty of Maybe you should talk to someone

Do you think meaning is more important to people or is pleasure more important?

Who do you miss in life?

Does one person in your life remind you of someone else?

Chapter Forty-One of Maybe you should talk to someone

What do you think of Rita's progress? Why do you think Rita doesn't care about the progress she had made? Do you think that perhaps she feels that her recent developments don't make up for a lifetime of failure?

Have you ever been jealous of someone with more stability than you?

Why do you think Rita has a hard time forgiving herself and being compassionate toward herself? This attitude is likely the source of her suffering.

| |
| |
| |
| |
| |
| |
| |

Chapter Forty-Two of Maybe you should talk to someone

How often to you worry about being liked?

Chapter Forty-Three of Maybe you should talk to someone

What have you learned from Julie and her advice?

Chapter Forty-Four of Maybe you should talk to someone

Why do you think Lori changed her mind about her ex-boyfriend? Why does she no longer consider him a bad person?

What do you think of the ex-boyfriend's email?

Do you think Lori should have cancelled her book contract?

Chapter Forty-Five of Maybe you should talk to someone

Why do you think Wendell changed his style and his office so much?

Do you believe Lori is attracted to her therapist?

Do you ever dwell in bad emotions or do you tend to examine them?

Do you think Lori is finally starting to heal?

Chapter Forty-Six of Maybe you should talk to someone

Do you think Charlotte is being avoidant?

Do you have any lingering issues from childhood that still show up in your life today?

Chapter Forty-Seven of Maybe you should talk to someone

Is there a hierarchy of pain in society? Do people constantly compare their pain to the pain of others?

Chapter Forty-Eight of Maybe you should talk to someone

How do you feel about John's emotional side and his wish to honor Gabe's memory?

Chapter Forty-Nine of Maybe you should talk to someone

Do you keep any secrets in your relationships?

Did Lori do the right thing by telling Wendell that the wife of one of her patients sees him?

Chapter Fifty of Maybe you should talk to someone

What do you think of Julie's idea to throw a party?

Notes and Reflections:

Chapter Fifty-One of Maybe you should talk to someone

How do you feel about Rita's long and emotional letter? Do you think this is a letter to her kids or to Myron?

What do you think of Rita's life story?

Chapter Fifty-Two of Maybe you should talk to someone

Have you ever displaced your anger onto anyone?

How can Lori live life fully and not worry so much about her health?

Chapter Fifty-Three of Maybe you should talk to someone

Do you believe that the therapist character in John's show is based on John's therapy treatment with Lori?

Why do you think the character of the show is becoming more humane?

Do you have a hard time being vulnerable?

Chapter Fifty-Four of Maybe you should talk to someone

What do you think of Rita's life now?

What do you think of Rita's relationship with her kids?

Do you know anyone who has struggled with depression?

Chapter Fifty-Five of Maybe you should talk to someone

What do you think of Julie's desire for wanting her husband to find a new life partner?

Was it a good idea for Lori to go to the funeral? What do you think of her experience there? Have you ever been to a funeral? Was your experience similar?

Who has made an impact on your life?

Chapter Fifty-Six of Maybe you should talk to someone

What do you think about John questioning whether he's an ass or not?

Have you ever wanted to accomplish something but life had taken you in a different direction? Perhaps in a better direction?

Chapter Fifty-Seven of Maybe you should talk to someone

Why do you suppose that Lori is now energized about her writing? Is it because her new book is more in alignment with who she is?

Are you ready to dance?

Do you feel that Lori is ready to end therapy?

Chapter Fifty-Eight of Maybe you should talk to someone

Which relationships in your life feel like they ended but still aren't over yet?

Do you enjoy sunshine?

Notes

Thank you for reading and writing!

We hope you learned something new and were able to learn more about yourself, reflect on your life, and relate to Lori's experiences.

We care about your reading experience here at Book Nerd and want to provide you with thorough and insightful book guides.

We'd like to give you a virtual high five for reading until the very end. You're a great reader!

Before we part ways, do you mind leaving us a review on Amazon? We would appreciate that greatly, and your support will help us create more book guides in the future.

Thanks again!

Yours Truly,

Book Nerd Team

Made in the USA
Middletown, DE
06 January 2020